PREFACE

4th November 2022 was t changed for Maia. While dressing gown, her life lit eyes as she lay in a ball o excruciating pain, bleeding from a brain haemorrhage. After calling her mum to come home and ringing the ambulance, she was rushed to hospital to have emergency surgery.

Having been told by the surgeons that the haemorrhage was an *'unlucky, random injury'*, Maia knew her hectic lifestyle of working three to four jobs, feeling burnt out and not having the time to rest or focus on her own passions could have been factors that led to that fateful day.

A few days before the brain injury, after a long twelve-hour shift, Maia clearly recalls saying to her mum, 'I wish I could just sleep for a week.' The universe answered her prayer but in the most painful and life-threatening way imaginable.

Finding herself lying in a hospital bed day after day, feeling increasingly depressed at the thought of not knowing if she would ever walk or be healthy again, Maia entered a phase of deep reflection.

She was drawn to explore the thirty-three years of her existence on this earth. Having experienced tremendous loss and traumatic heartbreak throughout her life, Maia was inspired to write thirty-three pieces of heartfelt poetry to honour each year of her life thus far, and so 'The Dressing Gown Poet' was born.

Influenced by the vibrant life of West London, where she grew up, each chapter takes the reader on an emotional journey of manifestations and magical memories that have illuminated the rights of passage of her life, her losses, her loves, and all that lies between.

Throughout Maia's life, she has endured a lot of loss, where many of her close friends were murdered through knife and gun violence, and she never really processed the grief until poetry came into her life. Maia also lost people to the tragic Grenfell Tower fire in 2017, where she witnessed the tower burning from her place of work and area. The anger and trauma that she and her peers felt during that time and still feel have encouraged Maia to speak the truth about the injustices and wrongdoings of the system—or 'shitstem' as she and her community call it.

From being so close to death in 2022 from the brain haemorrhage, Maia speaks of her newfound love of life, where she seeks beauty in ordinary, simple things. Through a lot of heartbreak from failed relationships, unexpected deaths and battles with sadness, Maia has learnt that in this hectic London life, where everyone is rushing and chasing money, we often miss out on rest, spending time with ourselves, loved ones and cherishing the natural mystic this world has to offer. The love explored in this collection finds beauty in the harsh lessons learned, showing the high and low energies of love where self-worth and gratitude play a huge part in healing our traumas as people and working towards a higher good, filled with great health.

Poetry resonates with Maia's life purpose, which is to be of service to her community in a creative way and help give a voice to others who may be battling with their own crisis. No matter what kind of illness, trauma, uncomfortable situations or stages of life people go through, Maia believes that we can still find the majestic radiance that life presents, giving us all a chance to step out of a sometimes victim low vibrational mentality and into a higher frequency allowing us to blossom. Choosing to bring delight to the mundane through spoken word helps Maia to shift and move through discomfort and gives way to cultivating confidence and being awakened with a glimmer of faith, no matter what's happening in life. Poetry gives Maia an expressive outlet to process pain and various emotions in a freeing, peaceful way where she can regain love and gratitude for the ordinary with wordplay, rhythm, music, writing and voice.

Give thanks!
X

FOREWORD

It takes a great deal of courage to find strength in our vulnerability. To consider happiness for ourselves in times of despair. To want better with faith in the knowledge that better can exist. To triumph as we prevail from our hardest times with a commitment to living.

Maia's ability to communicate her truth is a testament to her talent and purpose. This collection is both poignant and uplifting, honest and full of resistance. Advocating for change in our society, campaigning for an end to corruption and encouraging an uprising within ourselves.

This collection has undeniably been curated with the intention to empower others and it does exactly that. Maia immersed herself into her ARTiculation of her own life changing experiences. This collection is not only Maia's exploration of self but a testament to all of us who have had to adapt to the unexpected. It's a collection for the community, it challenges the constructs of society and demands change.

"The Dressing Gown Poet, Life, Loss and Love" alludes to the pinnacles of life whilst we look for life's meaning. The collection derives from hardship but is found in a state of comfort, with an appreciation for rest and recovery. Maia's work is a testament to the fragility of life and our fear of death. It honours the transformation that occurs when we feel loss in our lives and the healing nature of love. As well as the effect each component has on our understanding of self. This collection is for those of us who have had to adapt and reflect on their trauma for the sake of healing.

Poetry is clearly a form of self-expression for Maia. The healing these pieces offer for those of us who are ready to receive is beyond comprehension and exceeds expectation.

This collection has been carefully curated with consideration. It's an offering to conserve the well-being of the reader. Between the numerology and affirmations and the beautiful illustrations it's so much more than poetry. It's a poetic embrace, a reminder that you are held on your hardest days. An honest depiction of disappointment in a system that continues to fail so many. A profound narration of self-discovery. This entire collection is an ode for those of us who have felt the depths of our depression and dared to imagine a way out.

Maia's art acknowledges trauma, it testifies to our similarities and asks for solidarity in the name of love. This collection reminds us to be present in our own experience of life, to live with gratitude and kindness for ourselves and others whilst learning more about Maia as a person and as a poet.

Each word is filled with the humility that comes with learning to love your own life after loss. As you lose loved ones, your hopes, after you have grieved for versions of yourself. It demonstrates a deep appreciation of our fragility, the durability of the body and the strength of the mind. As Maia defies challenges and corruption she identifies the need for correction. Ensuring that this work is an authentic reflection of her values and journey to date.

By Yasmin Ali (Y.A Poet)

THE DRESSING GOWN POET

Life • Loss • Love

Written by
Maia J. Watkins

Paperback: 978-1-0686644-0-3
Audiobook: 978-1-0686644-1-0
Ebook: 978-1-0686644-2-7

A CIP record of this book is available from the British Library.

First paperback edition June 2024.

Cover art and illustrations by Sadia Zulfiqar

Printed by Maia True Living in the UK.
Maia True Living
London, UK

www.maiatrueliving.com

Acknowledgements

I start by thanking my precious mum, Yvonne Jackson-Browne, for always being by my side. You gave me life, you saved my life, and I am eternally grateful.

Up-full blessings to my family and friends (including those who have transitioned to the heavens). You have stood by me during every struggle and all my triumphs. Thank you for treading this earth with me. I love each and every one of you to the moon and back!

Love and light to Gwen Allison, who guided and coached me through the process of making this collection come to life, giving me the confidence to share my words with the world. The journey's been healing.

None of this would have been possible without my faith in Jah, my ancestors and the universe. Thank you for the beauty, gifts and experiences of my life and its many possibilities. I am highly blessed and highly favoured.

Contents

11:11

An abundance of blessings awaits us all.
At the end of every action, there is a promise, so worry less, smile more and don't give up.

The Dressing Gown Poet

AT THE TIME OF WRITING THIS, I lounge around, recovering in my dressing gown.
Thanking the Most High out loud, feeling blessed and proud to have made it out alive.

I spend most days at home with months off work, embarking on a journey of resting, replenishing and recovering.
Reflecting and contemplating on how precious life really is.
With plenty of thinking and profound analysis, I dive further into how I want my life to be.
Moving forward, you see, there are lots of changes for me.
I consider my purpose more deeply.

I didn't completely know what direction to take, so I wrote and created and now this collection's been made.

Thirty-three pieces of words and poetry.
I invite you to embark on this journey where **life, loss, love** are considered the main themes.

I am **The Dressing Gown Poet**.

Taking you on a voyage, exploring the realms of my world.
Just a girl from the ends, experiencing ups and downs like so many of my friends.
I have stories to tell with my pen, written through life's lens.

At 33, I faced death in the face.
Haemorrhaging on the floor in nothing more than the dressing gown I wore.
Naked underneath as the day I was born.
Bleeding in the brain, vomiting alone and torn.

I'm grateful to tell the tale, coming through blessed and up-full, no need to dwell.
But let me remind you of the truth.
Life's great but also a struggle.
It includes love and loss, filled with more to go as the years progress and we continue to grow.

The future is bright, but the paths aren't always light.
Life's a dance, a game of chance; there's no way to tell which path will go well.

I've lost close friends to murder, witnessed my community in flames.

Never forget Grenfell Tower; the dark memories forever remain.
My best friend gave birth in front of my eyes.
The strength and beauty left me inspired.
When life flashed before me, being a mother was what I desired.
I love life, and giving thanks is required.

This thing we call life is not what you expect.
Nothing is promised, predicted or set.
I've encountered true love, run into heartbreak and learned so much about the challenges we humans face.

On this manifesting journey, mental wellness is a biggie, so I practise self-love, remembering that health is the ultimate wealth.

I smile a majestic smile, grinning teeth in style, wearing my grey dressing gown.
The pink one I had for years has been thrown out—no tears.
It was old and carried memories of pain when I suffered bleeding in the brain.

I am **The Dressing Gown Poet** who loves to play with lyrics and rhymes.

The universe is full of miracles, leaving me speechless oftentimes.
A lot of discomfort, love and discovery.
Finding happiness in the ordinary makes life a lovely luxury.

This collection you read explores the fragments of existing and living.
Touching on the spirit of deep healing and forgiving.

Love and light X

12:12

I am overflowing with gratitude and I move gracefully towards situations that make my spirit and soul happy. Today and every day, I am thankful for being alive.

LIFE

Surviving A Brain Haemorrhage (Part 1)

Surviving a brain haemorrhage was no fun and games.
My whole existence was burning in flames, leaving me unconscious and drained.

The trauma in my brain left me confused and scared.
What if I don't make it? Will my life be spared?

Knees weak, arms were heavy, and like Eminem, I lost myself; the haemorrhage was messy.
Passed out on the floor with dread, feeling cold and sore.
I rang my mum to come home; I didn't wanna be alone.
The discomfort was insane, like fireworks being let off in my brain.
I'm glad the paramedics came.
My mum was the hero; if she hadn't come back in time, I'd be out of this game.

999, off in the ambulance. The paramedics had my back.

Morphine through my veins to ease the bleed attack.
CT scans, needles, and life flashing before my eyes.
If you were there, you would have heard my cries.

A Subarachnoid Haemorrhage is what I was told I had.
And the look on their faces, I knew it was bad.
Critical, in fact.
Subarachnoid Haemorrhage.
What kind of name is that?
Sounds like a spaceship, but I'm alive and glad.

I didn't feel elegant, especially in that medical gown.
I frowned, knowing I had a minimum of three weeks in Charing Cross' hospital town.
My life had taken a turn, and I was out for the count.
Keeping me alive was paramount.

Aunts and uncles prayed that the bleed wouldn't grow.
Constant beeping of the machines, my blood pressure was low.
I came around from the op, ICU is where I had to go.
Intensive care due to this brain scare.
I was trapped in this ongoing nightmare.

Parents cried, family and friends too.
I felt bad for panicking you.

The haemorrhage had been contained.
I had two rough procedures through my groin up to my brain.
The technology was insane.
Knives, wires and screens.
They did their magic, and my mum was so pleased.

The first procedure was harrowing like hell.
They injected dye into my brain cells.
I was blinded by the light.
Saw the colours orange and red whilst levitating on the bed.
This was dread.

Thank God for the main op I was put to sleep.
This injury was way more than skin deep.
I asked the surgeons:
'Will I wake up in one piece?'
Next thing I knew, I was fast asleep.
Didn't even make it to counting sheep.
The anaesthesia gave me that release.

Woke up with a catheter just hanging between my legs.

I couldn't tell when I was peeing, and every two
hours, I took meds.
My head was killing.
My new world, constantly spinning.

The recovery's ongoing and it's taught me to rest.
Not feeling guilty; it's all for the best.
This could be a test from God, I'm sure, because,
from a near-death experience, I now reflect more.

I've let life be a vacation full of electric energy.
Who knows what lies ahead?
I'm so done with the meds and their rotten side
effects.
Got my valerian tea and sea moss instead.

I'd taken tasks for granted, like walking and bathing
my skin.
I'm not superwoman, so I took the advice of getting
constant rest, in.
I felt so tired and down; it's not a crime that
recovery takes time.
I had to remember that it was the little things that
were the big wins in order for the improved life to
begin.
I'm lucky to be alive, that's all I'm saying.

During my time in the hospital, I experienced
cramps in my legs and pins and needles 24/7.
I couldn't walk for weeks.
Was my future still looking bleak?
I'd urge my brain to send telepathic singles to my legs, and I'd wobble and fall.
I felt exhausted and stressed.
My mind said: "Lift your left leg," "Now try your right."
I was doing the hokey kokey with a bunch of questions, fears and tears.
'Will I ever walk again?'
'Is my memory OK?'
'Please, no more migraines.'
Doctors surrounded my bed, asking questions:
"Where are you now? Can you tell us what day?"
Nurses checking up on me; 'Maia, are you OK?'

Once discharged from the ward and forced into
more rest, I decided to focus on my creative-ness.
I've written many poems full of life and things.
I've had some time to reflect and fly my wings.
I'm grateful to be alive to nurture my inner child.
A second chance perhaps, my heart beats, I'm haps.

I take nothing for granted.
I handle life with care, as some didn't make it, which seems unfair.

I witnessed a man in ICU transition to the heavens above and I prayed for his spirit to live on and beyond.
That night, I had the shivers. His poor family cried rivers.
One minute he was there, and the next, he was gone.
The nurses did their best, but he just hadn't won.

A few weeks later, I was healing OK at home, but suddenly, I was out of the zone.
I was feeling so sore, and I was rushed to the hospital once more.
Nose bleeds in the risings, I knew things weren't right.
The dizziness was back, giving me a fright.
I was vomiting, too, with a migraine in full view.
I couldn't take the setback; I wanted to get through.
88th in the emergency queue.
It didn't look bright.
Paramedics and nurses were all on strike.
My face was pale, looking very ghostlike.
I cried, holding my head.
Mum booked an Uber instead.
No ambulances were to be seen.
I was back in Charing Cross with more panicking.
I had waited and waited for the results to come in.

CT scans showed NO brain bleeding within.
My head felt strained, but my health was maintained.
I was relieved not to be haemorrhaging again.

These ups and downs could make me feel paro, but I trust in God that I'll see tomorrow.
My mental health's been tested, yet I stay up-full and rested.
No stress for the blessed.

One day, I'll look back on that brain attack.
It will be a distant memory that taught me this and that.

This experience is something to tell my future kids.
That mummy soldiered the near miss, continuing to lead with love, gratitude and bliss.

Every day, I wake up and pray, trodding safe and sound on the journeys I take.

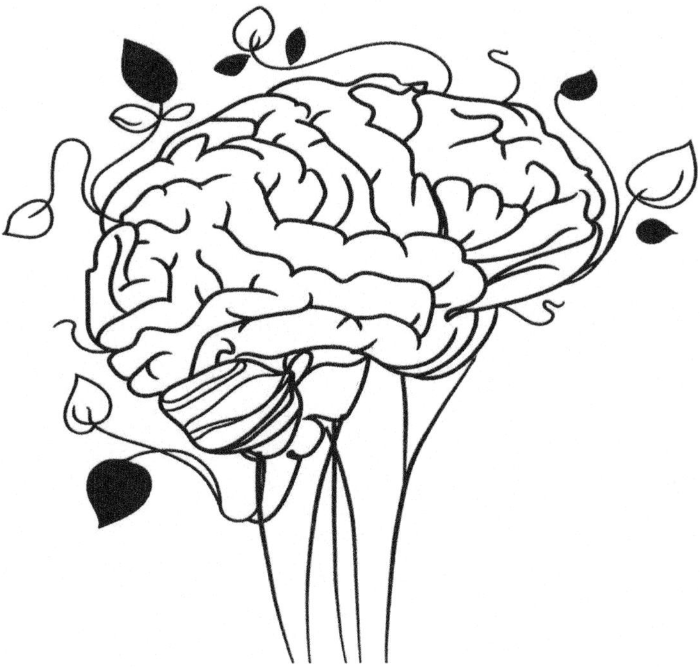

33rd Year

33.

Free Free.

The year of creativity.
Spiritual abundance.
Love, laugh and dance.

Thirty-three years in this current life so far.
Number of the master teacher.

Major breakthroughs.
Learning, exploring and healing too.

Self-expression and the manifestation of the higher self.
Health is wealth!

What life are we creating?
What life are we activating?
Consistency and discipline, the world is liberating.

All things are possible!

33 THINGS TO DO.

Get through three a day if you want to, especially when feeling down and blue.

1. Make your bed
2. Exercise and stretch
3. Eat healthy, tasty food
4. Drink plenty of water
5. Declutter your space
6. Go for a walk
7. Dance
8. Have a relaxing bath
9. Practice gratitude
10. Meditate
11. Read a good book
12. Listen to music
13. Listen to a podcast
14. Set a goal or intention
15. Take social media breaks
16. Spend time with family and friends
17. Make a smoothie
18. Play and create
19. Get enough sleep
20. Give yourself and someone a compliment
21. Put your diffuser on
22. Have a lie in
23. Rest
24. Write one thing you love about yourself

25. Make time for reflection
26. Do something out of your comfort zone
27. Journal
28. Watch a good show or film
29. Cry if you want to
30. Choose and repeat an affirmation
31. Do something you've been putting off
32. Buy a plant, plant a plant
33. Take a deep breath

33 years + of growth,
enlightenment & blessings

Slumped, BUT I Got Back Up

Why do I feel slumped?
Sometimes…
Emotionally drained.
I just can't explain, but at times, I'm in pain.
A pain that's not felt via cut or bruise but a discomfort that's mentally engraved.

Some risings, I wake up, even bake up, wanting the day to work in my favour.
I aim to stay healthy and grounded like a strong tree.
This world can trap the spirit when all I want is to be free.

Life can be hard, real tough and dark.

A wave pulls me under despite my wants to stay afloat.
I'm sinking.
Sometimes…
Down.
Girl down.
Man, I feel down.
Am I drowning?

Or suffocating from a cold grey cloud immersed in gloomy gas?

Depression.
A low, long, lasting mood.
A poison.
Not how I imagined.
It's not great.
I choose to meditate.
To write.
And journal.
Breathe those negative doubts away.
Breathe in 2, 3, 4…
Breathe out 2, 3, 4…
Repeat 2, 3, 4…
Yes, it's a huge chore…
It feels like a world war.
Depression 2, 3, 4…
My mind needs caring for.

When the journey is hard, I do not fear, for Jah is near.
All may not be clear, but I persevere.
Remaining grateful and somewhat brave.

Letting go of the 'I can't do this'… (Yes, I can).
'I'm not good enough' …. (Yes, I am).
I let go.

Freedom.
Finally,
Today.

With a slight smile in my eyes,
I exhale slowly,
Experiencing miracles.

Healing.

A tiny twinkle of hope stops me from hiding away.
Today, I release myself from under the duvet.
Curtains open and I let in the sun's rays.

I'm up!
Taking each moment as it comes.
Just for today, I will not worry.
I'm healthy.
I'm alive and ready to face the day.
I am excited to play, no matter what challenges
come my way.

I was once slumped and sometimes still am.
BUT I got back up.
I swear we all can.

Raise Our Vibrations

No crazy baldhead men can run we.
We don't fear them; we have all that we need.
Truth, love, but never ever greed.
Believe in yourself, that is key.

Even if others are too blind to see,
No propaganda, we need clarity.
But remember young ones...
Leading with love is what keeps us free.

There are too many crimes against humanity.
Racism, wars & human trafficking.
Ten times deadlier than the 'Rona'.
It's insanity… politricks and savagery.
We move forward with love and not brutality.
Listen to the teachings of His Majesty.
Sitting comfortably with a cup of herbal tea, we stay up-full.
Leave a legacy.

Raise our vibrations,
Seek liberation,
We focus,
Meditation.

Hold our heads up high to the sky.
The world is our oyster now, let's all fly.
Young ones, stand firm in your truths; make sure you believe.

Choose love over money.
Let's use our wisdom.
Working together, escape the system.
Have ambition.
Be the master of your own mission.

Slaying the vampire, we roam like lions.
Troding together to reach our Zion.
Bounce back despite the setbacks.
Bounce back despite the setbacks.

Raise our vibrations,
Seek liberation,
We focus,
Meditation.

Reclaim our energies and build memories.
Our hearts and minds stay clean.
Look to the sky and connect your third eye.
Message music.
No excuses.

Remember your worth.
We have to believe.
Let's sit and unwind as goals come to mind.
Full enjoyment.
As things now align.
Our souls......are never being sold.

We have to believe.
Believe in yourself.
We have to believe.
Believe in yourself.

Always...
Young ones...
Stand firm in your truths, and make sure you believe.

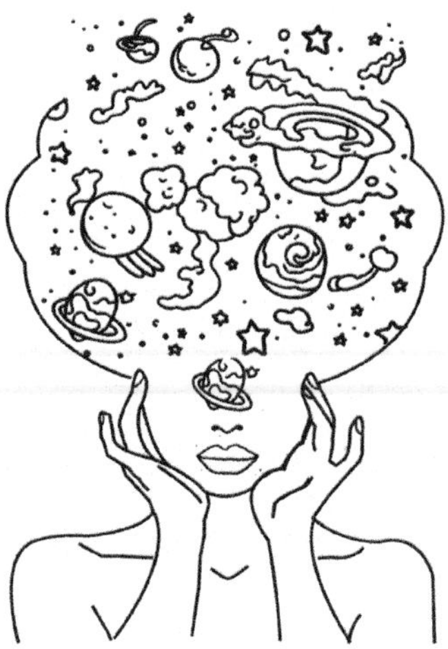

13:13

I rise above all
limitations and keep my
sights on my purpose.
My soul is ready to
ascend to new,
beautiful heights.
Forgive and be free;
everything is going to
work out.
I allow love to fill my
body, mind and soul.

LIFE - Part 2

Justice. Peace. Freedom.

Justice.

Justice is fairness and equality.
A chance to take responsibility for our actions as human beings.
Justice is doing right by the universal laws where truth, balance and harmony become the major keys to upholding a righteous society.
Justice.
Justice is doing right by the karmic laws.
Justice.
Justice is nature.
Justice is unity.
Justice is closure.
Closure for those disturbed by the wrongdoings of others.
The wrongs which have caused immense pain and suffering.
Justice represents a moral principle.
A principle that every living entity deserves to be protected.
A principle that everything, in theory, is treated fairly on this earth that we cherish so dearly.

Peace.

Peace is restoring that balance, truth and victory.
It's the master key to connecting with the Almighty.
Peace is a form of happiness.
A meditation.
A blissful sensation of a community's vibration.
Peace is security.
Peace is being uplifted physically, mentally and spiritually, feeling at ease without the notions of greed.
Home is peace.
A place to reside and feel stress-free.
Peace is the understanding and acceptance of self.
It's living without fear.
It's mastering a positive spirit with no regrets, just lessons learned.
Peace is having harmonious relationships with the I, others and nature.
No violence or hostility lives within peace.
Peace is chill.
Peace is a state of well-being amongst a timeless silence of up-full thoughts and feelings.
I like peace.

Freedom.
Freedom is chance, choice and opportunity.
It's abundance in wealth, health and love.
Freedom is not being enslaved or failed by a system created to hurt you.
It's independence with no constraints.
A break from chains.
Removing the mask.
Freedom.
Freedom is the right to speak and the right to act.
Freedom is seeing clearly and simply, activating the third eye to grow wisely.
Freedom is stability and liberation.
A chance to use your voice and find purpose.
Freedom.
Freedom is being ready to take on any challenge.
Freedom is education, growth and gratitude.
Freedom is flying.

Justice, peace, freedom.

Sweet Bali

The adventures begin as I travel solo within this
world we live in.
Bali, oh sweet Bali.
An Indonesian island - known for its beautiful
beaches, volcanic mountains and iconic rice
paddies.
Forests for days, temples we give praise...in.
Island of the Gods where spirit meets culture and
earth meets paradise.
Backpacking freely.
Travelling solo got my crystals with me.
Malachite and pyrite but I ain't no fool.
The golden rule is they're protecting me whilst I
sightsee.

Gaining insight into daily village life and meeting
locals on the way; they invite me in for Balinese
coffee.
Sweet, holy aromas, high vibrations.
Smiling faces everywhere, offerings amongst the
air.
I give gratitude, thanks and praises to the Most High
and neighbours.
One heart but many Gods for different life
elements.

Supreme karma.
New moons and full.
I learn about the creators of all things great.
The rulers of heaven, earth and universal states.

I explore the many cafes and markets around the town.
Pure hearts as I trod amongst Balinese grounds.
Delicious spices, sandalwood incense.
I sit on the road with a cup of ginger lemon tea.

The mood is fly, but I try not to catch a look in a monkey's eye.
These cheeky beings, all shapes and sizes, are a part of Bali's surprises.
I've entered their home; I'm in their zone.
Watch out, though. These smart creatures will steal your phone.

I embrace the Balinese ways.
Watch a traditional dance driven by human chanting and trance.
Rhythms changing, fires burning, stories presented.

Waking up in Bali on Christmas day, what can I say? I'm ready to play.
Never thought I'd see the day when I'd learn to ride a bike.

I embrace the challenge of rolling down hills.
My balance is off-key, yet I'm enjoying the thrills.

Sideman Bali next to Mount Agung.
A new favourite place, full of nature and open space.
Incredibly green and quiet.
A hidden, untouched gem in Bali.
Morning walks, family temples, water palaces, I'm in my element, my soul balances.

I eat lunch with my hands, intensifying my connection with food.
Food served in banana leaves.
Food with new textures heightens my mood.

The journey continues to Mount Batur.
A curiosity about volcanoes has come to light.
At 3 am, a new moon, I climb this beast and catch the sunrise with all its might.
I'm with a team of solo women, torches at the ready.
We keep a moderate pace, surrounded by dark space.
I'm out of breath and sweating.
Who knew this climb would be so testing?
We weave in and around stony trails and up steep, slippery hills.

Volcanic rubble, believe me, you don't want to slip,
so we keep a firm grip.
Then, three hours later and after moments of rest,
we reach the top, and I'm well impressed.
Words cannot describe the magical beauty deep
within my eyes.
Breathtaking pinks, purples and blues spread
through the sky.
I feel high.
I begin to cry, no word of a lie.
This has to be what paradise looks like.
I'm proud of myself for climbing such a wonder.
My fear of heights no longer exists.
I said, 'Yes!' to something that scared me, and
glory is what I saw.
That night, I smiled peacefully to sleep.

Fruit and veg markets are on my list.
I'm surrounded by many.
I love them all.
Flavours burst, and I'm able to explore.
In every corner, there's so much more.
Pink dragon fruits, its fluorescent-coloured flesh.
Mango's tropical, nevertheless.
Smelly dorian, spiky and free.
Oh, how I adore... Bali.

I've become this peaceful warrior trodding via indigenous plants.
Beachfront walks and beachside restaurants.
I watch the final sunrise of the decade with new friends.
Everything's nice, no pain, just blissful gains.

New Year's Eve and I enter the serene jungle.
Bali Eco Stay is where I lay, breaking into the New Year with wishes for a brighter future.
I watch a burning lantern take to Mars, disappearing between the stars.
My open-air Garden of Eden is where I sleep to the sounds of a running stream.

1st of January.
A three-hour trail with a recently found American friend.
And also a random stray dog.
We find waterfalls and get drenched in the showering rain.
Hot stone massages in open-air huts.
I hear the echoes of gushing water and distant sound gongs.
That feeling of 'Om'.
Experiencing peace, soul self within.
I'm always searching, forever learning.

So bright and awake, this heavenly feeling
overtakes me.

New vibes as I cross the ocean to Gili Air.
Spontaneous boat rides where the Indian Ocean
meets the Pacific.
Wavy.
I snorkel bravely and find huge turtles.
My favourite spirit reptile.
'To be like a turtle is to be at ease in my own shell.'
Music on deck, the vibes are in check and the
ukulele is played live and direct.
Smiles, laughter, flirty eyes.
I love these moments; I'm mesmerised.
Island life is definitely for me.
Going with the flow, so blessed and so free.
No one can ruin this journey for me.

My solo adventures are coming to an end and yes, I
tried SO hard to extend.

Now, welcome to my boat ride from hell.
Gili Air back to Bali.
Madness.
I'm leaving, so I guess the heavens are full of
sadness.
Waves for days as this packed boat sways.

Side to side, up and over, I'm going through a vomit
phase.
Rough winds where the grey clouds meet the
boisterous sea.
I wonder what will become of me.
Hopefully, I make it back safely 'cause, boy, this
boat is way too shaky.
Bumpy motions over coral reefs.
Nothing surrounds me except the everlasting sea.
Free me from this journey.
I just want to be back in Bali already.
Sick bags passed around as I wrote all this down.

The trip has reached its finished line.

Goodbyes are not forever.
They are not the end.
Bali, I'll miss you until we meet again.
I'm thankful, inspired and honoured by all those
I've met.
Of all the things I've seen.
Oh, sweet Bali.
This place holds a special love within.

P.S. I've developed an obsession with Balinese doors...

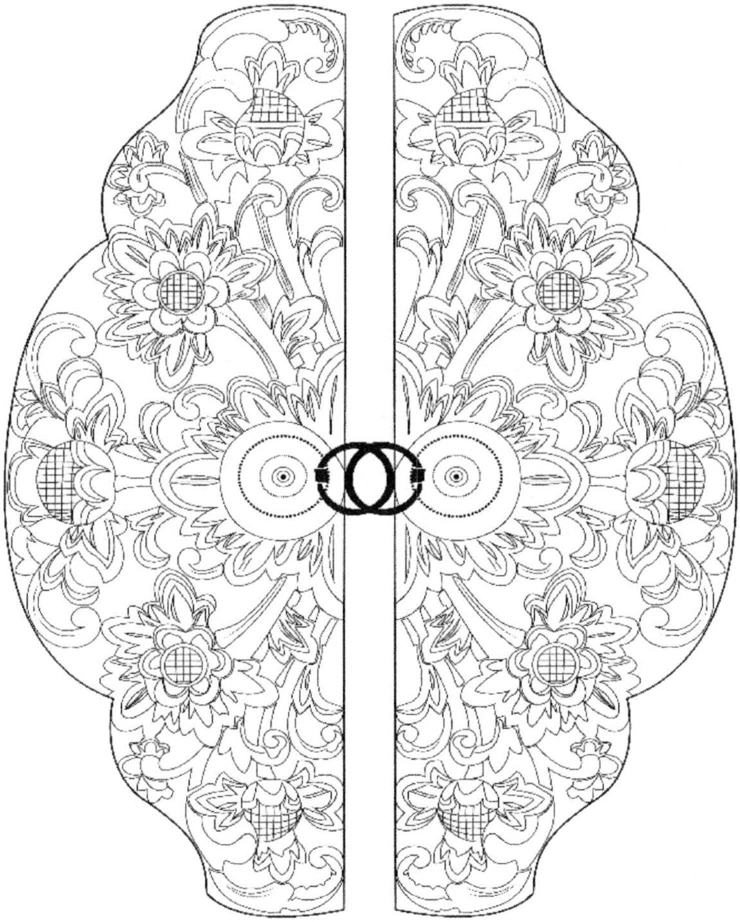

Am I Angry with the World?

Am I angry with the world?
Or angry with the people occupying it?
Maybe I'm just a misfit.

If only humans would learn from their history
instead of repeating the same tormented misery.
Everyone knows war isn't the answer.
Yet thousands of years later, people are fighting,
killing, abusing or avoiding.
Not caring.
A lot of hating.
This shouldn't be the life we are creating.
That's why I sometimes feel angry and often debate
things.

I try to free the mind from depression and the
constant mental weight.
I won't be blind to the love I know feels so great.
The world is a beautiful place.
Let it be, let it live, let it breathe and develop
naturally.
Treat it with care.
Like a baby.
Nurturing is the key.

Don't kill it or each other; we’ve got to work together.
Respecting one another, my brother and sister.
I’m open to what's around me.
The moon and the sea.
I’m not angry with the world when I feel safe and free.

Happy and kind.
Don’t get left behind.
Seek help and give help to those in need.
Am I angry with the world or with people and their greed?

Life’s about sharing wisdom, teaching the youth and breaking down unjust systems.
Vexation and anger are creating blocks.
Holding us back from the healing of breathing.
We’ll break cycles and find greatness.
Together, let's hate less.
I’m not angry with the world but with the people who cause stress.

Nourish the mind, forgive and give.
Let love be a shield and guide.
Moving forward, what is the vibe?
Always protect the I.

Forever a student.
Grateful for what I've got.
The world is our oyster; explore it, don't stop.

Am I angry with the world or just consumed by fear?
I ask as many of us are anxious all year.
It's difficult to know what to do.
There's a lot we all go through.
Cost of living crisis.
Lack of funds, too.
Inflation rising.
Bank balance's crying.
Working three or four jobs to make ends meet.
You can see why life gets so peak.
We don't take the time to sit back and unwind.

Let's face our fears.
Don't be afraid.
There's a lot to be angry with, but the world is not to be blamed.

Grateful

First things first, give thanks to the Most High.
The One who created I and I.
Grateful to be truly alive.
Making conscious efforts to strive.

Doing what I love most.
Yet, I turn down what doesn't serve me.
My spirit carries thee; I'm carefree.
Honestly.

Ready to take on life's challenges.
I learned to manage things whilst staying talented.
Balances and balancing.
I just wanna survive and win.

No more carrying a million plates.
Running here, there, to every workplace.
Settle myself; it's not up for debate.
Celebrate the glory that awaits.
Forever grateful but never hateful.
I have life and health and my belly is always full.
Mum's cooking.
What more could I ask for?
Fresh juices, smoothies galore.
Rice and peas.

Dumplings.
Plenty of coleslaw.

Yes, I nearly died, but I got the universe on my side.

I'm so happy and grateful for my family and friends.
That's not where the story ends.
I'm grateful for the seasons, freedoms and love at first sight.
Reasons to sleep in, with you by my side.
I thank the moon and stars that I didn't just die.

Holidays and happy ways keep me grateful, always.
Autumn leaves, the rain and the breeze.
Appreciate all I experience and see.
Grateful, oh so grateful. I thank you, God, for saving me.

Give full thanks to the Most High,
The One who created I and I.

Let life be full of Love and Light.

14:14

I am excited to be here, right now, in this moment. I surrender to what I cannot control. I make decisions based on who I am becoming. Liberate the mind and freedom will follow.

LOSS

A Nation of Constant Abuse

As we guide each other through the revolution,
I see us marching for justice, peace and solution.
Burning down corrupt constitutions.
I notice the hatred in some people's eyes as we trod on by.
Black is beautiful. No lie, stay praising the Most, Most High.

Walk safe, family.
Remember that racists don't like you and me.
They ain't worthy in any degree.
Breonna T, R.I.P.
We don't stand for police brutality.
It's time to escape thee.
Raise your heads up to the sky.
They can't erase history.
My brothers and sisters stay up mentally, physically and spiritually.
These holistic three are all we need to break free.
We can't fight the fight if we're unhealthy.
Keep the heart and mind clean.
Never bow down to their racist regimes.

We are Black Kings and Queens, so only take the knee when necessary, like Colin KP, as we pray for more than just equality.
We are no longer invisible.
We don't apologise for our blackness or give way to the modern KKK.
Silence is violence.
Educate ourselves and those around thee.
Buy black and support the community.
It ain't that hard, honestly.
Do better since black lives definitely do matter.
Every black man, woman and child, it's our time to smile.

Too many of us are being murdered, too much bloodshed flows across the globe, and the constant violence going viral through our mobile phones.
It messes with our royal melanin psyche.
This can't be all that our children see.
Their eyes were once innocent and totally free.
A nation of constant abuse, stop desensitising all ah we!

You whipped us for years across our backs.
You lynched us from trees because we're black, and now you kill us in our streets and homes as we struggle to breathe while you crush our bones.

The hate you give makes it hard to forgive.
These profound grounds were built by so-called 'slaves' from ancient African towns.
We are not slaves.
We are spiritual entities born from a lineage of ancient warriors, majestic storytellers and royal heroes.
Our basic human rights should not come at a price.

We are black.
We are proud spirits.
We have a right to life, liberty and security.

Respect us is all we say and keep your violent behaviour far, far away.

No More

Please
No more.
Please redesign your minds and stop with what we call 'knife crime'.
We ain't got the strength to be digging more grave holes and grieving these lost souls.
Poor mothers can't heal, can't turn back time as they sit by their window's wishing for a sign as to why their son's life was stolen.
Hoping there's some mistake and praying for little man to come home as she stares through the glass, trying to stay brave.
But she's hurting and deep down, Mummy knows her son ain't returning in the same clothes he left in.
He ain't walking down that same London Road alive and composed.
He's gone.
It's unbearable to see a mother bury her young.
To witness families being ripped apart by grief, uncles gritting their teeth, hungry for revenge, it can't go on.
Something's got to be done.

Communities need to strive for better whilst working together.

We all have the stuff to get off our chests, but instead, we hit the roads and put on those stab-proof vests.
We're paranoid and shook for our lives and I get it, cause you don't know who the hell is carrying a knife.
None of us were born to be bad, and we certainly weren't born to be killers.
So let's use our wise brains and allow the hype because deep down, we're all the same.
We're scared.
We're heartbroken.
We're traumatised and we've somehow lost our ways.
So, please…
No more.

Please, you're too young to die.
Too young to fly to the skies with other passers who pass you by like angels in the clouds.
We ain't ready to be angels.
We wanna grow up, have a family, fulfil our dreams and make something of this particular life, so really deep this and deep it right.
Our young ones are being murdered all through the night.
I've lost too many people over the years.

Nearly lost my brother in 2018, aka my bestie, my twiny twin twin.
Who are you to think you can take another person's life?
Who are you to take away a family's precious jewel?
Who are you to rip the life out of a fellow bredrin, a fellow sistren?

Stop doing those in the system a favour by making their lives easier as it's one less 'working class' kid living.
One less 'refugee' kid progressing.
One less 'black' kid excelling or learning or simply breathing.
They love this so-called 'black-on-black' violence.
And I quote 'black on black' coz it's not just black people killing black people.
It's more than that.
The media keep twisting it, saying it's only black kids in London that carry knives, but if you travel the UK and other parts of the world, you'll see it's just the same, but they don't call it 'white on white' violence.
They just call it violence.
So, what's the difference?

You were all just babies born free from chains, but now all that is left are blood stains.
You weren’t meant to die before dawn.
It ain't fair, youthful ones.
Know your worth and let’s all begin to position ourselves within this universal realm we call life.
Earth.
This place we call home.

Just know you are wanted.
You are loved and you are cherished.
Every single one of you, so please…
No more.

I get it may not feel like it, especially when all people care about is Brexit and it's bullsh*t.
Spending money we ‘supposedly’ don’t have on government bonuses and war crimes when we need to use this ‘supposed’ money on the youth.
The youth clubs that have provided conscious activities for our youth, apprenticeships, schooling, sports, holistic health, the NHS that have saved our youth, saved my brother and the list goes on.
And on.
And on.

We understand that it’s tough times as we trod through these rough winds, but please keep breathing, young Kings and Queens.
Remember, you are special and you are worthy of life.

Milad

There are days when I'm fine and then, out of
nowhere, you spring into mind.
The way my heart aches as I picture your face,
remembering that you are no longer here.

I never got to say goodbye or hold your hand for the
last time and kiss you goodnight.
I love you, I always will and I know wherever you
are, you'll be alright.
You've got the angels looking after you, deep, deep
in the sky.
Continuous bliss, a soul kiss and no more pain as
you rest in eternal peace.

My vision of you fades and your image slowly
strays from my mind.
I don't wanna forget.
Or lose sight of you.
As time flies by since your passing, I struggle to
picture your face as it once was, as it would be if
you were still here with me today.

I put pen to paper as a teardrop drops, smudging the
ink.

I desperately try to picture your whole self like it used to be.
I'm sad that I'll never hear your laugh again.
One thing is for sure: I'll remember your smile and I'll smile.
Smile through the highs and the lows as I picture your kind eyes.

Memories blur over time and the flickers and flashes take over my mind with faint snippets of what used to be.

When I feel down and lonely, I know I've got your presence with me.
Your spirit lives on via the flowers, trees and soft winds.
You didn't make it to 30, but your existence lives on for eternity.

In this big, wide world, as the universe aligns, things fall into place even though you've transitioned and are flowing through space.
I can feel your energy around me like electric pulses shifting through my veins.
You've retired from this realm, leaving family and friends behind.
Just know we love you and it's time for peace of mind.

I miss you with all my heart and soul.
Wishing for one more moment, one last laugh.
One more second so I can say my farewells.
But in reality, I know this will never happen.
Things have to restart, but your memories live
within me forever in my heart.

15:15

I invite miracles to
happen in my life.
I am magnetic. I am
drawing in everything
that I desire and need to
prosper.
Claim those big plans
that the universe has for
you.
A grateful heart is a
magnet for miracles.

LOSS - Part 2

The Mourning Bird

Saying goodbye to a loved one, a young one, a precious son.
Navigating our way through the deadly silence of loss and trauma.
Our King's spirit soldiers on through sweet memories as we rebuild and heal.
Life seems unreal.
Let's aim to make good of the world as our tears water the seeds of our one-day future happiness.

No mother, brother, friend or foe should feel this deep and lasting sorrow.
Right now, our hearts stay hollow.
Someone is missing.
God, if you're listening, stop us from witnessing our young ones disappearing.
Our communities need repairing.
Help us conquer these senseless acts of violence on our streets.
Weep if you must; our hearts have been crushed, and our souls mourn as life feels so unjust.

Walk safe, youthful ones and know how it truly feels to be alive.
Be winged with purpose and light.

It'll be alright if we all unite.
Free from pain, with only love to gain.

Like a beautiful dove, you fly.
Blessed King, you are the carefree winds that blow amongst the trees.
You are the sunlight that shines through your mother's window.
The stars that glisten as you remain your brother's hero.

If words could reach our lost one, we'd tell him we love him.
We'd place kisses upon his forehead.
We'd hug him tightly.
Our aching hearts speak freedom and justice.
Without the answer, death feels cold and corrupted.

But we know it's you passing through the world's view when the birds fly overseas.
Rest in eternal peace you are now so, so free.

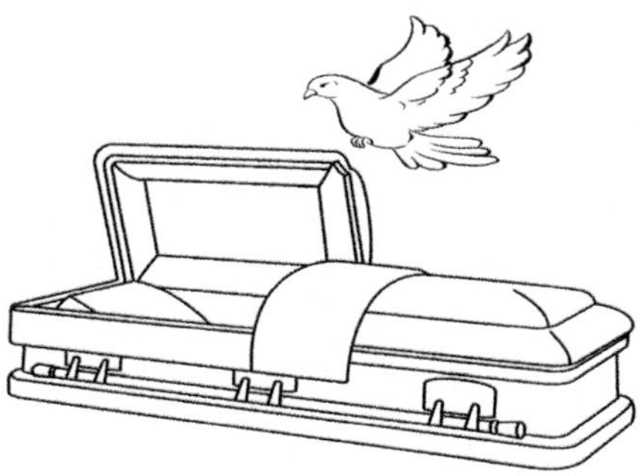

Insomnia - Part 1

Tired.
Constantly tired.
I just can't sleep.
I'm counting sheep.
Heard it helps.
I ask myself, 'When I do sleep, do I really sleep
because the sleep I do get doesn't feel like sleep?
What is sleep?'
Sleep… A sedentary state of mind and body.
Several hours.
Gives the nervous system powers.
Eyes closed, muscles relaxed, dreaming peacefully,
keeping my organs intact.
That is the sleep I want to attract.

Sometimes, it feels like I've closed my eyes for one
second, then BOOM!
My alarm goes off.
Other times, I wake up suddenly.
BANG!
Shit.
I fell out of bed.
My head... my head.

I find myself sweating, breathing heavily, thinking
my teeth have fallen out.
It's a recurring dream. A nightmare.
I'm looking in the mirror and I've got no teeth.
Someone's ripped them out of my gums one by one.
This constant feeling of anxiety can't be undone.
Fearing the future is no fun.
I'm a hot mess.
Stress.
Beginning to discover bags under my eyes like I'm
65.
Most people get eight hours of shut-eye.
Eight hours of delightful dreams.
Waking up feeling utter bliss.
But me… me... I'm just tired and pissed.

Insomnia - Part 2

Insomnia.
Part 2: no sleep, what's new?
A regular disorder that makes it hard for me to sleep, to stay asleep, to not wake up constantly….
Man, this is deep.
I am so tired.
Physically drained but emotionally awake.
Creating a headache.
Ffs.
Overthinking.
I don't know what to do.
Waiting for some sort of breakthrough.
I'm ready for bed.
I really am.
Got my routine, my new sleep program.
I turn off my lights, my TV and my phone.
Close my eyes.
I feel alone.
I lay exhausted and wide awake all at the same time.
I try hard to force myself to sleep.
I smoke a spliff and drink some mint tea.
I listen to soft rain sounds as I hear it helps.
None of it works for me right now.
I count sheep.

AGAIN.
123456... I get to 100 and realise it's long.

I lie awake, looking at my ceiling full of glowing stars.
The night becomes the morning and one by one, those stars disappear.
Oh dear.
I haven't slept in days and I’m in a haze.
Sounds crazy, but it's possible.
This current obstacle.
I hear the birds chirping and cars driving by.
Kids going to school—insomnia is cruel.
I look at my phone.
I’ve gotta be up in an hour.
It's 6 am and I've had no sleep.
The story of my continuous week.

This can't be life; changes need to be made.
What’s the next stage?
A good night’s sleep seems so far away.

The Flower of Rage

The drilling keeps me awake as I try to sleep and rest my soul.
My tender petals wither away from exhaustion.
Dehydration as the castration continues, becoming louder and angrier.
I cling tightly to the vibrating ground.
In the depths of hell, no love is found.

Earth's existence.

My roots are decrepit and frail.
I long for clean air that I can inhale.

Shattered nerve endings.
I am torn apart with a brittle, broken heart.
A battered system.
Shockwaves of debris rip through me painfully.
Breathing deeply, I try hard to alleviate the pain.
Chemtrails, coughing, I can’t take anymore.
I look up at the polluted dust particles and I scream and roar.

I travel to an environment which was once full of life.

Green meadows and vast landscapes have been cut
with a knife.
Homo sapiens creep up on me… slyly…
They think of themselves highly.
Crushing the remains of my steady, strong frame.
No comfort here, just constant wear and tear.

I'm the last of my kind, no place to call home.
I weep as a venomous bitterness builds through my
system.
No peace or love surrounds me.
Just heartbreak and solitude in this sterile, dusty
realm.
I was once free, growing beneath a giant fruit tree.
Now the tips of my lifeless leaves and once
beautiful flowers lay limp, clinging to my stem for
dear, dear life.

I want to pierce and poison the next mortal being
that I come into contact with.
Everything is ruined and grey.
Just let me fly away.
I howl, but nothing or no one can hear my dismay.

Mourning the destruction of my being, I feel so
easily forgotten.
My raging tears bubble through the distressed earth.

Mother Nature wets her baron soil with sullen tears of grief.

What have humans done?

My seedling entities are no more.
No fertilised love will happen here.
No matter what season, nothing will change.
When will the drilling stop?
There is no end.

I contemplate those heavenly sunsets.
Where graceful winds caressed my soulful being.
Lovely, victorious days where strong flowery scents of lavender and rose arose from the ground to bless those all around.
Delicious aromas fill my being with love, but the drilling creeps in over and over again.

My now uncomfortable journey to finding safe refuge has left me fighting and fragile.
I am so full of rage.
Why wasn't I left alone, in my home, peaceful and calm?
The divine sweetness of freedom that I previously had; roots rotten bad, I’m constantly sad.
All dreams have been stolen and ripped to shreds.

And like a child having tantrums and strops, my
anger builds and never stops.
Trapped in my own depression, I wither away.
Overthrown by weeds, my life gives way.
I am The Flower of Rage.

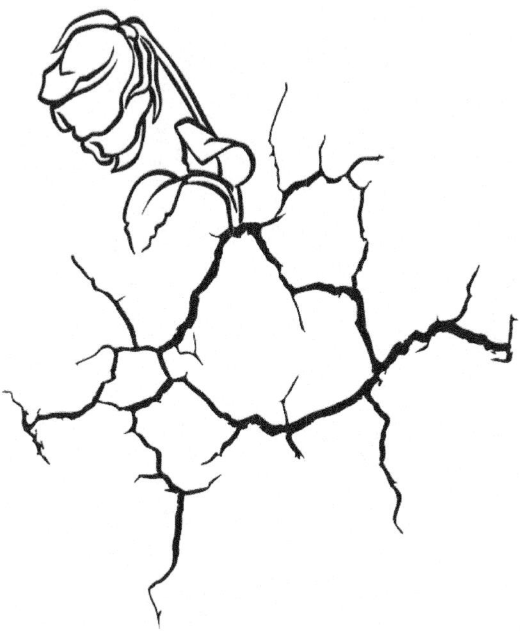

16:16

I release all habits that
are disempowering.
I am releasing blame,
taking responsibility for
my life and reclaiming
my power.
I am intentional with
my words, thoughts and
actions.

LOVE

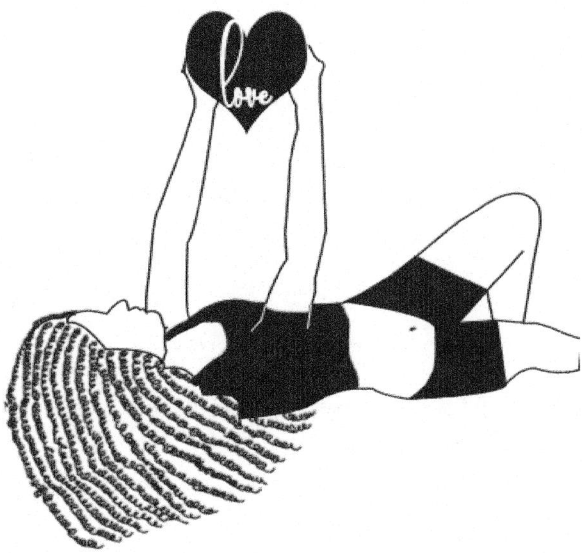

Paragraphs of Conversations

Brudda is fineeeee…
I'm caught up, yeah…
I am, no joke.
This man is a mood.
Like he'd just fallen from the heavens.

We stand, smiling at each other.
Weird, I know, but hey.
Feels like the universe is connecting us forever today.
Yey…

I love the way we talk back and forth daily.
My heart's doing a madness, fanny flutters, butterflies, you name it.
Flows of dialogue elevate each other's vibe.
We're inseparable.
Everything with you is pleasurable.
You are my shining star; nothing could break us apart.

I see WhatsApp messages pop up with your name, and I beam.

I'm beaming at the first line of positivity, real shy when you call me babe, laughing when you tell dry jokes.
Your words uplift me when I'm down and hiding.
We talk about everything and everything, nothing and nothing.
You got me blushing.

I think deeply before my replies as I take in your precious words via WhatsApp and texts.
I'm curious as to how you came to be and what attracts you to me.
You're intelligent, spiritual and simply beautiful.
I don't just mean beautiful in looks, you know!
Your spirit turns me on as our souls connect via paragraphs of conversations.
Late-night phone chats, pillow talks, dreams, the dialogue forever flows as we get to know each other's highs and lows.
Rah… I didn't know I could rhythm like that.
Love.
I'm in love.
I love intertwining your hands with mine.
I love reading over our treasured conversations, grateful to be a part of your thoughts.
I'm in love.
Humbled.
Our relationship is easy.

A sense of infinite vibration runs through our
bodies, inspiring our souls.
This is goals.

We don't ever go to bed angry at each other.
No drama, never a dilemma.
Only admiration and respect.
Peace and good sex.
Real good.......

Our serene dreams were never disrupted despite
your snoring.
The King and I want a family.
An extended reality.
We laugh at the idea of tiny feet running around in
our extremely tiny gaff in London.
In time we'll move to a place with a huge, huge
garden.
We visualise family holidays, messy bedrooms and
kids' football matches in the rain.
You love rain.
God knows why.
You love footy, too. And other things... Boo.
Nature, cooking, music...
We dance around the kitchen every strong-end,
bussing jokes, cheeks hurting.
Everything's working, just pure flirting.

Beloved blessings.
This is what success is.
The late-night talks and being with you, I’m happy and new.
Those paragraphs of conversations, blissful sensations, our breathtaking connection flow like the wind on a stormy afternoon.
Pure love, light and laughter.
May we continue to bloom.

Pole Poem

This is a pole poem.
A poem about love and pole.
A poem about dance.
Freedom.
The divine feminine, confidence and class.
Laughing upside-down, spinning around.
No frowns.

This is a pole poem.
A poem about love and pole.
Empowering the heart and soul.
Fitness and flow.
My happy place, if you know, you know!

This is a pole poem.
A poem about love and pole.
An art, an expression, a sensual addiction.
Inspired by music, core strength and endurance.
Keeps me flexible and adventurous.

This is a pole poem.
A poem about my love of pole.

I Miss This Guy

I miss this guy.
Despite his lack of communication.
I miss this guy.
Honestly, the frustration.
I miss this guy, his tender kisses and calm persona.
I miss this guy.
He’s even met my mother.
I miss this guy, although he ghosts when things get stressful.
I miss this guy.
But I deserve way more.
I miss this guy; his soul shines so bright.
I miss this guy, his deep voice and beautiful wide smile.
I miss this guy, especially when he's shy.
I miss this guy.

Do I stay or say goodbye??

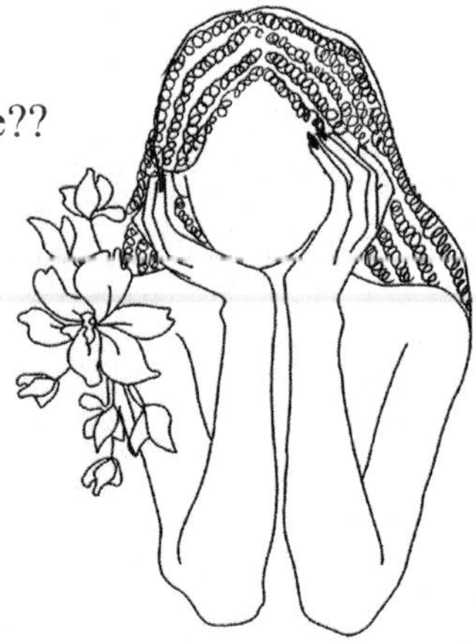

What If?

Don't wanna sound soft or in my feelings, but I
miss you.
I really do.
To the point where I think I'm falling for you.
Safe and sound when you're around.
Don't like to fight…
No battleground.

You're not much of a talker, so I rest in your
silence.
We both need a little guidance,
To express ourselves sincerely…
Clearly, we deserve a breakthrough.
You have me and I have you, but there's still some
work to do.

I often think:
'Is this boo bothered…?'
'Does his love run true…?'
He often thinks:
'Is this boo bothered…?'
'I wish she knew I love her too.'

Your cuddles are the best, so warm and safe.
Staying with you and going to bed late.

I somehow manage to sleep well, well.

I like listening to your breathing; I like the feeling.
Your heartbeat is healing.
Slowly, I drift off.
Peacefully.
I keep dreaming and believing.

Why I write this, I do not know.
I guess honesty helps to let love flow.
No holding back, no regret kicking in.
Communicating is better than not saying anything.
Verbal or through writing in pen.
I shouldn't be forever wondering…

What if you feel the same?
What if you don't?
By writing nothing, I'll never know.

So, my sweet darling, here I go…

17:17

I give myself grace
while I am growing and
learning.
I love myself through
the highs and lows.
I will not stop working,
creating and dreaming
when the journey gets
hard.

LOVE - Part 2

Love of Life

The many things I love
Of
About
In
Life…….

Adventures
Animals

Beginnings, middles and endings
Blessings
Breathing
Bravery
Belief and believing
Being

Children
Celebrations
Creating
Crying

Divine timings
Dreaming
Discovering

Dancing

Energy and energies
Exercising

Findings
Freedom
Family
Friends
Food
Fruits

Growth
Gratitude

Honouring
Hellos and goodbyes
Heartfelt moments
Holidays

Ideas
Insects

Journeys

Kissing
Knowledge

Love
Lessons
Learning
Laughing

Magic
Miracles
Mystery
Memories
Manifesting
Music

Nature

Opportunities

Prayer
Purpose

Quality
Quietness

Realness
Risks

Senses
Sacredness
Solitude

Spirit
Second chances
Sex
Smiling
Sharing

Treasures
Thoughts
Trial and error

Unity
Unlimiting

Vitality
Vibration

Wisdom

X-factor

You

Zestfulness

Life Partners

Play fighting in the bed…

Sheets.
Sheets rip beneath me as you give me deep strokes, you…

Looking into each other's eyes intently.
Watching.
Me looking back at you as you touch me softly.
Making my body want you more.

When I'm not with you, I want to be with you, touching you, kissing you.
We like chilling, too.

In each other's thoughts.
I feel caught by your loving vibes.
We're closer than before, which is more than I can ask for.
Sometimes, there are no words, no smiles, no laughs.
Just a gentle kiss upon my head as you hold me tight, deep in our bed.
No feeling of dread.
Only love and respect.

You, hunny, give me butterflies; my solar plexus shines, goosebumps as your lips touch mine.
A moment, a pause, a connected gaze, we are together, my friend.
Forever, the love stays.

Two souls intertwined within, breathing exactly as we embrace.
Touch skin.

Our bodies create this magical flow.
We become waves of the ocean.
My mind focused only on you.
I let go of everything.
All fears and worries disappear.
Our love is clear.
We ride together like rapid waves, drawing me further away from those terrible, painful days.
No more suffering.
No more tears.
Just you and I making sweet love.
Cheers!

Nothing else matters.

My King, your Queen, we take each other in and embrace life's world winds.

Sadness flees both of our minds as we feel each other coming.
Becoming.
Come like one body.
One heart.
Pulsating beats racing as we climax to the stars.
Far away into another galaxy.
Another realm.
A new paradise where we lose our minds.
Together forever.
Souls touching, relating, loving and more.
Fighting passions, a wild attraction, sparks beauty and freedom.
Everything will be alright.

You have saved me and put meaning to my thoughts.
I am protected.
We are connected.
Alive again with more happiness to gain.
Life partners.
Our love is everlasting.

Self-Care

Self-care.

Self-care protects our mental, emotional and physical health.
It's the real version of wealth.
Self-preservation.

Self-care is revolutionary.
Add it to your diary.
It's not selfish.
It's a basic need.
A chance to catch a break and recharge.

Self-care can look like solitude.
There's strength in being alone.
It's looking after ourselves.
Reading a book from the top shelf.
Listening to our favourite tunes.
Dancing.
Life-enhancing.

During a plague of anxiety and depression, we are feeling it and experiencing it.
Trying to keep up with the pace and stresses of daily life.

Rushing here, there and everywhere.
Not taking a breath or pausing to think.
Many wait for Friday to hit the bottle and drink.
Drowning with fear and doubt.
This shouldn't be what life is about.

Not practising self-care could be considered
madness.
Take time to chill and release any sadness.

It shouldn't be a luxury to be healthy.
Let's take the journey of self-discovery.
Self-care is there to prevent burnout.
Get plenty of sleep and eat good food when you
can.
The meaningful gift of self-love will increase our
lifespan.
Appreciate you for you and be gentle with the I.

Baby steps to the life we all desire.
Don't wait until we retire.

Take one day at a time.
Goals can't be met if we're unwell.
If the mind is not right, it can be hard to excel.
Self-care makes us feel warm and alive.
Giving us a chance to thrive.

Let's appreciate ourselves and invent our own world.
Self-care is a cure, and we deserve to be held.

I AM [.........................]

I am worthy and deserving of amazing things and experiences.
I am mentally, physically, spiritually and emotionally healthy.
I am talented.
I am the master of my wealth.
I am financially free.
I AM FREE.

I am surrounded by love and good people.
I am thankful for friends and family.
I am attracting high, vibrational love and soul healing.
I am inspired, and I inspire.
I am helping myself so I can help others.
I am strong, resilient and in control of my destiny.

I AM A LIVING, BREATHING MIRACLE.

I am in a righteous place, at the righteous time, doing the righteous thing.
I am BLESSED.
I am protected by the Most High.

I am a creator.

I am breathing in relaxation. I am deserving of rest.
I am ENOUGH.

I am a motivated, empowered, bold, growing and prosperous being.
I am doing my very best.
I am mastering the art of manifesting.
I am prepared for my wildest dreams and desires to come true.
I am open to receiving unexpected opportunities.
I am full of positive, loving energy.

I AM GRATEFUL FOR THIS MOMENT.

I am happy and hearty.
I am brave.
I am loveable.
I am attracting unconditional love.
I AM LOVE.

I AM… [insert name]...

18:18

Keep going, keep rising, keep believing in the I and the Most High.

I am inhaling great health and bringing peace with me wherever I go.

I attract inspiring and healthy people into my life.

About the Author

Born in West London to loving parents, Maia J. Watkins is a Rasta who practises Reiki and lives a very spiritual way of life. She is also a prolific actress, poet and author.

Her creative endeavours started at a young age when she began acting at a local youth centre after school to overcome shyness and make friends in her community.

Maia found herself captivated by the magical versatility of monologues, which allowed her to bring stories to life in her own unique, artistic way whilst having fun with rhyme, emotions and audience participation.

Having won the coveted 'Monologue Slam Award' three times in the UK and for the LA edition, Maia gained confidence in her abilities, which encouraged her to dive deeper into her passion for both poetry and acting.

Maia has shared her artistry with young people in schools, youth clubs and those who have unfortunately found themselves in and out of prison or pupil referral units.

Through creative writing workshops, performing arts and poetry, Maia encourages the young to have fun, build confidence and feel empowered in a safe, explorative and innovative way.

Maia has collaborated with two other accomplished artists and together, they perform the complex stories of young people living with HIV. Due to the stigma and battles they face, performing their experiences on their behalf through poetry gives young people the chance to have their voices heard on a global platform where the misconceptions of their illness can be challenged and used to educate others.

Choosing to delight in the mundane through spoken word helps Maia to shift and move through discomfort, giving her a way to cultivate confidence and be awakened with a glimmer of faith, no matter what is happening in life.

Poetry gives Maia an expressive outlet to process pain, sadness and various deep emotions in a freeing, peaceful way where she can regain love and gratitude for the ordinary with wordplay, rhythm, music, writing and voice.

To connect with Maia or to find out more about her activities, visit her website:

www.maiatrueliving.com

Printed in Great Britain
by Amazon

45270445R00066